KiRA

Isabe l l & th.

KIRA♡5♂

KiRASNotSoEs

Flower

by Moira Butterfield
illustrated by Paul Johnson

LITTLE SIMON
Published by Simon & Schuster
New York · London · Toronto · Sydney · Tokyo · Singapore

A little seed falls to the ground.

It might have been dropped from the sky by a bird.

Perhaps the wind blew it to its new home.

Perhaps an animal carried it.

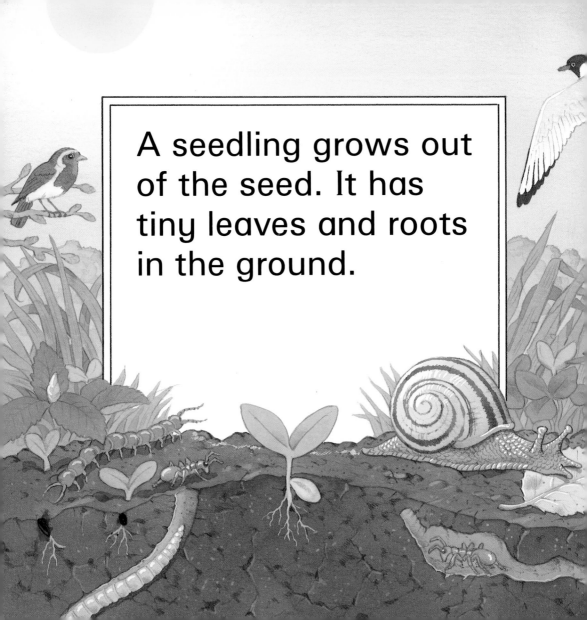

A seedling grows out of the seed. It has tiny leaves and roots in the ground.

The seedling needs sun and rain to help it grow taller.

The seedling grows into a plant with lots of leaves.

Soon the plant grows a bud. Inside there is a flower waiting to bloom.

The flower opens in the sunshine. It has a store of sweet nectar.

A bee comes to collect the nectar. She will use it to make honey.

The bee's coat gets covered with dust from the flower. The dust is called *pollen*.

The bee carries the pollen to another flower.

It rubs off her coat.

When a flower has been given some pollen, it can start to grow fruit.

Some fruits are soft, like apples and blackberries. Some fruits are hard, like nuts.

Some fruits have seeds on the outside.

Some fruits have seeds on the inside.

Soon the seeds will fall to the ground, ready to grow.